Devil's Paintbrush

DEVIL'S PAINTBRUSH

Desirée Alvarez

BAUHAN PUBLISHING
PETERBOROUGH NEW HAMPSHIRE
2016

ISBN 978-087233-218-8

Library of Congress Cataloging-in-Publication Data
Names: Alvarez, Desirée, author.
Title: Devil's Paintbrush: poems/Desirée Alvarez.
Description: Peterborough, New Hampshire: Bauhan Publishing 2016
Identifiers: LCCN 2015049315| ISBN 9780872332188 (pbk.:alk.paper)
Classification: LCC PS53601.L877 A62016|DDC811/.6--dc23
LC record available at http://lccn.loc.gov/2015049315

Devil's Paintbrush is the 2015 May Sarton New Hampshire Poetry Prize Winner.
www.bauhanpublishing.com/may-sarton-prize

Book design by Kirsty Anderson.
Typeset in Bembo Book MT, with titles in Michael Harvey's "Strayhorn."
Cover design by Henry James.
Cover image: "Flamethrower" by Desirée Alvarez (desireealvarez.com).
Author photo by Robert Herman, and used with permission.
Manufactured by Kase Printing.

BAUHAN
PUBLISHING LLC
PO BOX 117   PETERBOROUGH NEW HAMPSHIRE 03458
603-567-4430
WWW.BAUHANPUBLISHING.COM

MANUFACTURED IN THE UNITED STATES

CONTENTS

Trompe l'Oeil

Djinn   12

Echolocation   13

The Lace Makers   14

The Order in Which Things Are Broken   15

If the War Goes Very Well   16

The Art of Bell Ringing   18

Early Explorer's Journal   19

Night Vision   20

Indian Elephant   21

Amor Fati   22

Shame   23

Portraiture

Scrapyard   26

Restaging the Battle of the Litte Bighorn   27

Counterspell   28

The Piñata Maker   29

War Doll   30

Essay on What Father Really Does for a Living   31

Grace   32

Pilgrimage   33

Mysterium Tremendum   34

Aria   35

Three Great-Aunts Gardening   36

Great-Aunt's Diary   37
Lesson in Chiaroscuro   38
Abstraction is Enchanted Ground and I Have Something
   Terrible to Paint before Harvest Time   39

Night Landscape

Sakuramochi   42
The Trouble is that We Make Night   43
Vagabonding   44
Blood Mandala   45
Minotaur, Moving   46
In the Garden   47
Whale Light   48
Before the Garden Grew   48
Letter to the Chief of the Weather   50
Chorus of Snow Quartz   51
Lake Lillinonah   52
She Loves Me, She Loves Me Not   53

Figure-Ground Illusion

Erased Drawing   56
The Inside of My Mouth   57
Andalusian   58
Mentor   59
The Contents of the Falconer's Bag   60
Arributes of Speed   61
Piranesian Space   62

Kitsunetsuki, the Fox Possession   63
Ingenue   64
Ingenue 2   65
Christina's World   66

Illuminated

What the Oracle Says   68
Confidence   69
Yours, in Snow   70
Under the Altar   71
Flute of Sugarcane   72
Tapestry of the Six Senses   73
Familiar   74
Shoebox Diorama   75
Intima   76
Music for Surrender   77
Giant   78
Pavane   79

Notes   80
Acknowledgments   81

for Mom
best friend & muse

Trompe L'Oeil

Djinn

When I was the warrior my hair hung blackly below my knees.

I studied the service that is the blue holding the sky.

At sixteen I shed the turban, cut my tress and gave it to mother to wear.

She will know what to do when it's coiled at the back of her head.

What is hard is hacking off the face from desire.

I was moving between two camps.

I have stayed too long in places unvisited by monsoon.

In all my time here I've seen only one cat.

I remove my hands from the wire hive of sleep.

I am afraid of myself.

I always leave the lights on in my chandelier.

After many hours flaming, my body begins to shake with the thousand bulbs.

I dip them in the sweet water of burn

where every night my steel knife puts the river to sleep.

Echolocation

It is the shortest night of the year.
The owls will return early.

A childhood without the attribute of a father lasts a lifetime.
Abandon, knock-kneed and erratic rules.
To know the moment you turned.

I stole the owl's nest that she stole from the hawk.
Since then I've always walked as though hands ran
up my legs and this is flight.

The Lace Makers

I ask my students what is the most beautiful thing they've seen.

Then I ask my lover.

He says, *a lacemaking convent in Bruges secreted behind walls.*

Devout women lived there after the men fought and died.

Houses in a row along the green. The brick roofs crenellated.

Hear the clicking of spools in deft hands.

See their grey heads bent to the finery.

Knuckles darting with bobbins. Fidelity.

Hadewijch of Brabant, the thirteenth-century mystic nun writes—

who loves gladly, remains.

In proportion as love grows, fear. Two fears about love.

Who is not worthy. Who cannot content.

Max Born began his theory of crystal lattices at the outbreak of war.

He and Einstein exchanged many letters of things they found beautiful.

The beginnings of molecular theory.

I want you to understand the way I think, each said.

Responsibility en masse does not exist, merely that of individuals.

Never let the right hand know what the left is doing.

Reciprocity is an incomplete description.

We have gone to the limit of an infinitely thin world line.

At the center of each sister's round table grows

the white fractal of a lichen blooming.

The nuns are whispering a prayer.

Someone is answering in thread roses.

How to behave—do not cease to surrender.

The Order in Which Things Are Broken

Ancients threw the masks down the cenote—
the faces smashed first in little ways before
the long drop, an eye or an ear broken, a mouth snapped
in half. Then, lifted from the well, two thousand years
later, still grinning and golden. The loose spooling of two
people fast unravels—how we let go of time spent,
how heat fades, how a body forgets fully what it knew.
I have learned your face as you will never.
The third day we met you gave me all your secrets
until I held an ocean in a cradle. Now all I ask for is more.

If the War Goes Very Well

Something more powerful than will,
the heart anarchic does not cease firing.

It has not finished sewing itself together.
What settles in the fine mesh:

longing. I am tame and used to loss.
The future puts its hands into my eyes

to fall into the human. Fast, we grow,
faster than bamboo grows, than a frog bleeds.

The limit of what I had follows me
to ocean bottom: a fish shadow pressing

the cabin door. This clinging to person
and place only to move on and under,

is it so with mammals and fish?
Contact sweeps across me every three seconds.

Sighted seaplane through periscope.
Sighted two seaplanes through periscope.

Surfaced. Sighted two planes, submerged.
Sighted the end, submerged.

Out there a great dark thing
will take none of the names I give it.

The Art of Bell Ringing

At his life's end, Roosevelt wears his boat cloak
for his last meeting with the king.

Old snow in the diorama in Diekirch never melts.
Soldiers in white bedsheets push the boat
night after night to the river crossing.

What is forgiveness. A smoking mirror
in the war museum, a yellow field of rapeseed spreading.

I no longer want to know the human names of things.
Children picnicking in woods under big trees
find the piles of metal helmets,

even boots with the tibiae of soldiers still inside.
They take home a basket full of bones.

Brancusi will not return to work at his anvil, carve oak,
broil steak at the stove he built. In his Paris studio
on a wooden bench rests the marble oval of a face.

On the Hudson River a boy writes his mother:
I am in a great hurry. I found two birds' nests. I took one egg.

Early Explorer's Journal

When they disembarked, the sound
of wild birds was deafening.
Of course, they would have to be killed.

When I cannot imagine the unimaginable
I know that somewhere someone can,
ruthlessly, passionate.

In the laboratory the young pigeon looks
into the cage's mirror to become female.
This is the meaning of beauty.

I bought a cage and drew a pair of eyes
to put inside, hanging from the perch.
I look at it for hours.

Prophecy of opposites: they cause each other.
If a thing becomes worse, once it was better.
How freedom can be understood.

Great-grandfather called all the birds to him
sitting in the garden, blind and listening.

Night Vision

I never felt so close to the moon, all the animals look

naked in the woods. I have no place in the sparkling.

They hire me to draw each thing before they kill it.

Tonight I am the turtle's draftsman.

Small, beloved world.

In labs they measure fear.

The thread wound around my ring finger

reminds me to the stranger inside dying to get out.

Indian Elephant

Her decorated head.

Her violet-painted feet pacing the ground of the temple.

How long she must have trained to take the money

gently with her trunk to pay the man with the stick.

When I give her the banana she gives it to the man.

Nights my lover does not spend with me

I learn to let myself out of the house

to watch the pearls of gulls string the abandoned pier.

White noise possesses the dark city, a life spins from the fisherman's line.

What is this I swim in that is not water?

In the snowman's prophecy, the monstrous and the beautiful

hover as one hat over the hazard of sunrise.

Amor Fati

Our romance is born within three rings.
Underground, the first ring, is the setting forth.

In your arms my rose scents the room
to press orange against the windows.

In the second, sadder ring, we wear mantles
of mothers and sons, ones left behind,

while all the animals who are our other selves
mark the walls in skins of accident and fear.

The third ring is the limpid world of horizon,
liquid as ships wrought of waves,

birds hatched of water. Pieces of old
dragon lie along the shore for us

to wear as the armor, heavy and mirrored,
in which we were born.

Shame

As if I did not know the secret inside the moth's
dingy wings is the blue of the cornflower.
We build our lives around the shapes.
The chair from van Gogh's bedroom,
Ensor's masks, Botticelli's diadem.
I stare at Titian's flayed faun, willing
the old master's thick brushstrokes
to be my own. I want to be fearless,
to not care about the after,
to be with the horses.
Between the wild and the mind, a long cry.
How can love replace habit as my refuge.
What we give up before beginning is dearest.
I have not been gentle enough to anything.

Portraiture

Scrapyard

Attention is the most I can give.

I remember where I came from.

A greasy metal scepter hammered in a dark garage.

I have been here before, standing in the cold workplaces of men.

A buck head, the lone beige high heel impaled on the wall.

Back when I didn't know I'd never know childbirth.

The few things I can do for a car. Tie up the muffler. Oil change. Body work.

The photographer addicted to not missing anything.

Thick-coated outdoor dog gnawing.

I saw the limp from the machine that crushed his leg,

not the acres of melons grandfather picked.

The single time I met him he sat with pride outside his trailer,

squinting under an aqua sombrero of straw.

The moment to have back would be that one, to make sure of the color of his eyes.

Restaging the Battle of the Little BigHorn

Father, here is where I put you when I am lonely.

Scorched on a great tan plain.

High dust and the women screaming.

All last week I dyed my clothes the right color for today.

With a woman in battle, do men fight more bravely?

Childhood was you stabbing the space

between your fingers with a knife.

The voice you brought was heavy

when you draped it over me.

I saw an eagle this morning, ripping wings into sky.

I put my head on its huge shoulder

to know tenderness and no more.

With your mind I saw the white men

killing their horses to hide behind.

Counterspell

This is to keep out evil,
says the boy drawing an apparatus.

Patchwork of lasers.
The magnetic safety shield is of light blue crayon.

Then tanks, atomic explosives.
I tell him to make one tiny entry to reach the gold.

I would have made the treasure miniature
but he sketches a big yellow mango

hanging with a crown at the top.
I don't tell him what I read today—

about the dogs left behind in Chernobyl.
I do tell him a story about the matchstick girl

with lion-mad locks and trembling hands
building a firehouse of matches.

Remembering my own small fingers
reaching into the dollhouse to fix a calico curtain.

Before I knew the world was not in good hands.
Peacefully they sat at the dining table—porcupine, bear, mouse.

The Piñata Maker

Quetzalcoatl dries out in the many suns of Valladolid,
the dragon's body of Mexican newspaper stretches
to both ends of the little porch.
Inside the orange row house the bodies
of donkeys and bears swing from the ceiling hooks.
A boy wraps wet paper ribbons
around a waist that will be a mermaid's.
Next door, the *carnicería*'s caged white rabbits and chickens
blink in the twilight before dinner.

War Doll

When the soldiers came back they put
new heads on the old doll bodies.
This was a job, something to pass time,
a soothing of a kind. Maud wore a cap
on her head and a Band-Aid on her vinyl neck.
I do not have a child to remember the dead.
Human: skin at the bends of fingers,
bruises the meaning of limbs.
What kept me this week was the ice
that covered everything growing.

Essay on What Father Really Does for a Living

Father's gone between the walls

but no one knows why, only the dog

who growls at the flowers on the wallpaper.

He lives between the wind and the wind.

He wears our rift as scales assist a fish to swim,

but we wear it like water wears a whirlpool,

out-paradised in our home.

Mama says to set his place for dinner,

she says when a fork drops a man visits.

Silver litters our floors. Our pricked feet

blot valentines upstairs and down the halls.

Grace

In the city, spring burns its way out
of me any way it can. Mother, I've made
a list of all the lovely things you've done
for me so I can remember when I leave you.
The tiny fields of mandrake, the violet lawn
of fleabane where the deer stares
with enormous splayed ears. Up high along
the cliff live the animals with spikes who climb
the hickory trees. I could go anytime now
and it would not be about the afterlife.
I will not be limited to truth. My mouth
will be hard against your forehead.

Pilgrimage

They bathe in backwaters,
wear black mandalas to climb the mountain.

My mistakes are silver-dusted trees
surrounding the stonecutter's hut.

They pack my cheeks with ash and lemon
to pierce my face with long arrows.

Chain leashes attach me to them.
The mistakes I make are dogs

chasing each other on hallowed lawns.
I rinse them in sugarcane.

They tell me to wear the metal waist of blue fire,
to sleep alone in the bed that is also a ship.

I leave the seeds in the fruit,
all the pleasure suspended on the platter.

Some of us are only part human.
I have doubted myself.

I put something woman
in the box that cannot be opened.

Mysterium Tremendum

Mother and child, gilded and radiant,
you are the paintings I look at longest.
No men in the gentle madonna worlds.
Light blazes from the unknown into all
the mornings and nights
I do not have a child to hold.
Wide gaze and open mouth,
ideal boy, love unconditional.
See her hands cup tiny feet.
I hear all the bowed instruments
with their long necks playing at once.
Wholly other, bring me to the rim of full.
I cannot look into anyone's eyes.
Let love happen to me.

Aria

From the years I sang mother's songs my voice is too strong.
The shoulders of the men I've loved have all tilted
downward on the left side.

They move as birds migrating over a lake, a mass leaving
a place, bent on an ancient direction.
Your terror of your own heart fills my hands.

I'd hold down the ground and you. But still you'd abandon me.
Once I was dangerous, now I am afraid
when we come to a tunnel full of horses.

Wait for me—I've not acted out all the parts.
The last to play is radiance,
when the mouth carries the egg of a lark.

Three Great-Aunts Gardening

How many years three great-aunts slept alone
after days spent tending gardens,
nodding to weather.

What it is to weed. To be tender.

To be a woman holding a bird
as if she's lost her head
in the beam of light that is a river.

If I run out of apple time, wizen.

In a violence of digging
to put a plant in the rocky ground to grow.
To watch the earth for it

when the year comes around again.

One aunt ironed a different apron for each day.
I can almost hear them calling me—
if I run out of time.

All morning I pruned the winged trees,

spindles with rounded horizons,
tall branching habits.
Now they're finished burning red for the birds.

Great-Aunt's Diary

When I was grown and she no longer with us,
I searched for traces of her gentle hands,
her choir voice. I found her typewriter
in the toolshed. Long ago the house rang
with her striking the keys of the old machine.
A mustard jar lid holds the ribbon spool.
A bit of her daybook is still in the roller.
On butter-yellow paper she writes:

Heavy sky with new moon is a bowl
holding water. Day filled with inconsequence.
Looked for fabric to cover the potholders
I forget and roast in the oven.
Found remnants of velvet for the child's dress—
there was the little girl again.
While knitting, pictures come to me.
Vision of the walk we took with the stroller
to watch the brook and the cows.
The farmer told us if a cow should deliver
while in pasture she is likely to hide the calf,
thinking to give it freedom.

Lesson in Chiaroscuro

My student draws Leonardo's drawing of a hand.

Long-fingered, made for flying.

She paints a flock of hands lovingly,

as if her life depends upon it.

Fluttering sunset fingers, bound for cave and cloud.

Hands for touching metal and milk.

We talk about lines of life and death in art class.

Fence of barbed wire. Road of armor.

Air of spears. Jagged heartbeat on the hospital machine.

Sky is never the same again after Mona Lisa.

Sfumato. Smoky cigarette sky fuming behind

her in the landscape of meander.

Not the roof of desert stars the nomads burned in

blue and golden clay on the ceilings of their worship.

My throat is dry from chalk dust and speaking about the ideal.

Abstraction Is Enchanted Ground and I Have Something Terrible to Paint Before Harvest Time

A wheat field, the linen sofa grandfather sat on

before lying down to die. My brain holds more

than my heart and my hands, hungry and vast.

On the sofa he wears a crown of velvet and cardboard.

I am beside him in my princess dress, my feet

a world away from floor. Infinity surrounds us

and we don't know it in the last. The rest of my life

remembers him holding me high in Atlantic wind,

above sand stinging four-year-old legs. Choose

the richest blue for water, thirty browns for beach grass.

Blend into sky where tree begins and ends.

Night Landscape

Sakuramochi

I do not need to ask the monk how it is
on the edge of a sword, I know misfortune—

the white horn plunged in the horse's breast
slowly rinsing the world in frost. The garden

evolves, an animal dissolves, I long for all
I let go. Ice queenly, I apologize to absence

and it follows me, listening carefully like a
blanket in a cradle. April, we wrapped the

sugared beans in pink rice with salted cherry
leaf to swallow spring and keep it longer.

But when your hands leave me I know the time
between now and the daffodil's yellow gun

firing at the late-day sky. After you're gone
I carry my body about, bells in my mouth.

The Trouble Is That We Make Night

But there was a kind of startled garden.
The smell of petals rising and leaves setting.

Even in perpetual dark, flowers.
The taste of fennel rushes in.

We sell the coal forgotten in the cellar
to buy a horse, swindler seeds and glass

to build a trellis of unknown
conduct and custody.

We will go on saying and doing terrible things.
Love, address the five senses

from your greenhouse walls.
Bid each farewell as you put them down.

Rest their bodies, lithe,
where there is space enough for both of us.

Vagabonding

What did you do after you left us?
Moored boat trying to cross the severed river.
In the extremity of not seeing you,
a tunnel long as war, and garlanded.
Stay unaired, house of childhood, keep my early.
Back when I was being erased.
First the mouth, then each limb. How it felt,
forsworn. What lingered, entreaty.
Oracle, I have changed.
I no longer wait for the angels of firearms
to step from the drawing. I have rummaged deep
in the handwritten catalogs where the rows of throats close.
Don't shut off the lights of our city tonight,
I am painting it all. Bring the toolbox and the wolf-headed
jar of tears, I have not forgotten that the mad
design teaches how to look at it.

Blood Mandala

When I sleep the tiger comes out of the woods, dark and spectacular.
The tiger is the future thinking it is finished.

The tiger is the scientist driving with the vaccine beside him.
Each stripe tolls as he slips back between the trees.

Behind the trees are not more trees.
The dream stops behind my sleep. There is no rug in glorious

detail under the dream table in the dream room. No forest. No floor.
I have not yet learned how to keep all around me alive and well.

Minotaur, Moving

I took the ladder and a dead horse from *Guernica*.
A scar of music plays its march across my brow

while night curls coarsely around my neck.
I was the target in bloom at the core.

Always was the bright sun on my coat,
now I kick against walls of bone.

The ladder is for my lover who climbs slowly down.
I sweep the dirt floor and will not let her leave.

As she sways toward me, hands cupped full
of grass, I hang orchids about her throat.

Then, suddenly the sound of many hooves—
I will be tame.

In the Garden

Caught in the hydrangea's netting, I am stilled as if dead.

The car lights beam at my black spiral.

I wait for you with your suede hand and the scissors.

Smell me, oily as anchovy, streaking your one ungloved hand.

I slick your wrist, insinuate up your arm.

Admit, you have never been touched so.

All my radiance is netted.

Tonight is a braid from me to you.

Press the scissors to my body coiled in the mesh.

Snip the plastic binding, move slowly up my delicate neck.

My long sheath ripples as you loosen scale after scale.

The shock of my body so available.

Grip me hard, I curl to possess your hand.

Hold me to the headlight to be sure I am right.

Your fist is a medusa—fling me free to the hillside.

Whale Light

Masks cover the floor, a carpet of eyes and lips mouthing O, O, O,

as if the world might begin fresh for each tragedian.

I have gambled everything to be so alone.

I live in an Egypt of smoothest faces, long heads and the geese beautiful

where the snakes move to higher ground when we rake the dead.

No one has taken me inside yet. Stone, sensitive as feathers.

I watch someone else's child make her mother a bouquet of torn lily stems.

By the old tired sea I listen to be called across the risk.

Lamentation is the blueberry road too washed-out for picking.

May my dog always be at my side.

Before the Garden Grew

The past leans into the fountain
while I think of family, of things that matter most.
When sisters hold hands,
sit in each other's laps and play in the river,
where we visit a frog after lacrosse.
Every week watching it throb,
telling stories of being wet and ugly and why.
The river's watercress, the tawny dog,
the calls of the cedar waxwing.
Great-aunt always there to comb the knots from our hair.
To have childhood back to know what to do with it.
Wishes were a language still tightly coiled
when boys under the full moon
built fortresses of snow to keep the girls away.

Letter to the Chief of Weather

All night loudly you called
but I did not answer back.
For me at morning you left a chill
sheet across the spring crocus beds.
How it felt as a child, wondrous,
your power. Now a slender vase.
In the field under the pear
tree too tall for picking, tufted
high grass frenzied with bees.
Old tree for years dropping us gold.
Moss curbing the yew where I napped.
Animal, vegetable, earthworm chart
of land underground, mineral.
How nature. By what umbilical
are we tied to orchard's green
branches, to iced blue Scilla flowers,
until the body's frail shell eats
the earth, lips into her dress of brown.

Chorus of Snow Quartz

More wondrous than alchemy,
the white hills are radioactive.

The quarry that once burned with light
quickens now to a text of nutshell and stick.

The green's apparatus invisibly turns
the flowers to telepathy.

Lichen glows as if a place could be a lover.
Hear, all the growing speaks of integrity.

Maidenhair fern, most delicate umbrella,
what an effort you make.

Whirling and transient,
the unseen brain's logic comforts.

All the spinning leaves are telling us,
if there be boundaries to fire, if the heart's radio

flits between psalm and squandered,
if the woods fill with pillars,

then bring on the long rains.
Who wants a caress.

What says the steward of tree to the keeper of rock.
Be aghast, behold, feeling is difficult.

Lake Lillinonah

I bring all the landscapes I've seen to this one.
The frozen lake below me is a belly groaning.

Church bells of Winchester ring.
Jane Austen's tomb sleeps on the floor.
A chandelier of human bone hangs in the church outside Prague.
Ranthambore's leopard in the North Indian forest
returns to her cage every night.
I still hear the woman in the Tamil village
begging me to take her young daughter.

I summon them all here to my cold flatland
as companions in the strange comfort of sorrow.
The dog and I climb uphill over old Potatuck graves.

Night, come down and join us, it's snowing again.
Water, glinting in all your forms about us, I will never understand.

She Loves Me, She Loves Me Not

Did you study three centuries of storm

Are you thinking you know them now

Have you measured all the temperatures of surface, of sea, of upper air

Assimilated the data, validated the models, assembled the atmospheres

Were there uncertainties, anomalies, random noises, biases

How careful a watch did you keep

Will you make a better weather for the crops, for the birds, for the beasts

Was it all worth it

Extravagant and rash one, are you now wistful

Do you want to fasten back the petals

Are you thinking about the flower

How yellow was the center, how velvety the whorl

Can you still smell her rusty perfume on the wind?

Figure-Ground Illusion

Erased Drawing

The center of the braid stays
invisible. The world has a self
deep asleep inside extinction.
Ashen sun under cloud is two suns.
The entire day enters my belly.
So many ways to move our bodies
toward the miraculous.
Before you leave, loved,
press your face against mine.
Abandon holds my hands,
still I cannot make a shell.
My humanity is always in question.
The fish that looked dead flashes
from my palm into the river's winter.

The Inside of My Mouth

The deer who grows antlers like ladders to the sky
turns back, but the world is still here.

The turtles go into their shells to make night.
I know the inside of my mouth better than longing.

Humans risk, making me like them more than otherwise.
We can always make another one.

Objects become important, emotion is not named.
The world is still here, bleaching the want.

Andalusian

I have killed one of their kin and now they come
out of nowhere in bronze chains to carry him home.

The ant's holler of death must be as mother says:
all living things feel pain.

For seven days your body waited to be
borne away and we heard nothing—

we do not even know how you looked
in your hotel room when you died.

But they vanished you in a great hush
of suitcase and coffin before I could arrive,

so far after my childhood, darkly veiled in pageantry,
to dig up your bones and bear properly,

on a bier of cactus and arrow,
the long word.

Mentor

The eater of dreams comes when I am deep in the spiral of night.
Each time she shoots, the arrow grazes her wrist.

She will never be aimless, never need the assurance of things.
After a day of kill, she puts flowers on my eyes.

Her target is pocked like an old sunflower, more hole than color.
I lie watch in the tall grass, beside my fear of blood.

She will teach me to hunt, not mother.
The will goes on, lit from behind.

The Contents of the Falconer's Bag

One neck twisted, bouquet of wintergreen,
stolen bloodroot and trailing arbutus,
black-handed tree fingering the mist.
Behind me white branches feather my back,
little conquests fill my head with beating wings,
moss pressing my feet is softer than rapture.
Even as I flee I long for the one at my shoulder,
my eye stalks the dark air for you.
Now I do alone all that once we did together.

Attributes of Speed

That year we were historians of night, hushed with a luckless bounty.
That year our job was picking up bones and matted fur, misfit wilds

broken into a paved rushstream. I still wonder about the turtle,
refugee who lived in the median, his life bracketed in the breath-

held swath of in-between where extreme flowers and force grass
break the highway's spine. But we all know of stag, panic, whiplash,

kill. Flash of a thing racing through goldest light a last
time. Fall, the drive back to the city.

Prayer for fallen steelworkers—you say a bridge is a woman's
neck covered in lace stitched by blood.

I say it's an across—
the interruption filling the hidden with will.

Piranesian Space

Green begins again, too tender, not the green I want.

Letter unopened on the desk of the small round mirror.

The limit of certainty is its own comfort.

I wanted the place I could never leave.

Here is prison like the leaf's structure.

I steal increasingly smaller things, silver and gold jingles.

Tiny lavender clams. Shivery piles in the bedroom.

What winter does the purple come from in these hyacinths?

A white business envelope carrying the thrill of handwriting.

You said the Greeks found the tusks of woolly mammoths.

And thought they were the bones of giant men.

All night my shells call for their ocean in fleet, shrill voices.

The shipwrecked Spanish pony stares out to sea.

Tomorrow I'll send you a plan for an animal that looks like us.

Kitsunetsuki, the Fox Possession

She is the shadow of a woman picking seaweed in the moonlight.

She tells her son to find her in the forest.

She says, *carry me with you at all times.*

He says, *leave something behind*

so I know you want to come back.

The boy's hand reaches for his vanishing mother.

Her eyes and long foxy tail are married to the woods.

Listen, she whispers, *I call you and all the leaves turn.*

Ingenue

What were you waiting for

Why did you take the rides

Were you fearless

Who let the light burn at the top of the staircase

Then what shape will you take

Will the man walk through the doorway

How did you play all the parts

Were you visited in your sleep

Where were you when the shad tree blew its petals

Did you read his letters

Why did you hide the drawings

You did not know him then

Did you grieve

What proof do you have?

Ingenue 2

With each risk I became.

Mother stitched my prom dress on.

All shallows and willowy.

She will cut off the gown when I return.

Building child cities for no one to see.

By an old woman growing bliss.

Watching the river for the fish to spawn.

The women all wrote, *when are you coming back?*

I was tangling the marionettes in the attic.

I am still ravenous.

Christina's World

I am invisible crossing
prairie on arms and knees to be wanted.

Grandmother is out looking for barn eggs
and catching a rooster to pluck.

I have not played with the others.
Nor been downstairs to the cellar.

I feel the air around each tiny insect wing
I crawl near in the field of eyelash grasses.

I take a creature's breath away with fists.
The horizon is the grey apron I press

against my palms if I am the handler
of gravity chasing bright.

When the man appears to me
I go to him knowing his front is human

and his back is white-feathered.
He will lift me up into the black

cherry tree where the corner of the gold
cornfield is unharvested.

Illuminated

What the Oracle Says

Here is the hardest harvest,
here is fear of visitors uninvited.
Press close to the ragged chorus that blooms
once a year for a few hours only.
A white bud like an iris with bleeds of purple,
looking like the flower you want to be.
This March when it opens early morning
paint it quickly. Sew a man of silk
to carry everywhere you go. To touch another
is to leave home and not come back.

Confidence

Click, the oak groans, a head turns. The petals of the owl's face.

How long we look at each other.

What proof is there at the bottom of its grey chest.

The dog spots me on the wind before I appear.

Vision is the egg making its own nest.

We surround ourselves with things made for ruin—

ship of straw, paper hat, lace collar, daisy chain.

We name a machine gun after the blood-

orange wildflower devil's paintbrush.

Our hankerings stain indelibly as blue hands

printed on the bat's dream of happiness.

Along the way, we pass junkyards, chicken and grain farms,

handpainted signs for bloodworms and live bait.

We say what we grow is most important.

A town is called Viola with fields of new corn.

My love, we are the boy taking the milkweed pod

home from the field to remember his day in the country.

Yours, In Snow

You drove up with the elk in the back of the truck.
Already split in two. Her heart,

that you would eat, almost beating beside you.
Never mind, it was her eyes—

the urge of the flower to open.
So big and human you were lost.

The primal is most meaningful and less.
I have not wanted to come to the high place

where I remember what I couldn't have.
Salt, butter, tobacco,

the taste of being held.
The cat's up in the magpie's nest again,

filling the hawthorn tree with hunger.
Silver wolves have us surrounded.

Your eyes, smoked blue, are full of mountains
and something beyond that keeps me.

Under the Altar

I heard you say you were there
when they put the wings on the angel.

You saw the blood in its eyes,
the stains from the nails streaking the woodcarver's

door, the ship in full sail, clover and all
the true flowers for it to be May.

Inside me all the time it is snowing.
If myth is the part of the story that bleeds,

carry the rope to me gently not as a whip
but as an impossibly slender woman,

alabaster, and filled with perfume.
I no longer believe in the boundless

and the dog watches me
always now, but I still want you

to bury me so I can ride in the old chariot
of wild fig tree with oiled pigskin wheels

out of the kitchen bright into the next form.

Flute of Sugarcane

Never guess if the tiny bird the con holds is living or dead.

He'll let it fly or kill it in his clasp before he tells.

To wake from the stickiness of being human.

The city wraps me in its grey checkered coat.

Old lozenge to suck in its threadbare pocket.

I try to hold something all my own.

Inside me a salt lick square.

Hail out of season, corralling little iced hands.

We are already in the forgetting of glitter black waters.

The goose moves against the current tonight.

Only the land turtle sees the mayapples.

Forgotten for a heartbeat, the engines of siege,

when we bring a child into the world

we note how beautiful the world is.

Tapestry of the Six Senses

Teaching each sense
in its time is what mothers do.

You were the unicorn
in your tidy circle of gate.

The cowbell is ringing. She is calling me.

The dog skims the river
gently with the side of her face,
then lifts a drink at the end like a kiss.

The plants have leaves in their embryos.
Did you feel a part of the earth or apart
with their veins in yours?

Still smelling of field grass,
her hair in a locket.

O will you not come back to me now
if only for an hour,
my arms are wide as wilderness waiting.

Plant the grave with sea roses.
She will send up a four-leaf clover.

Familiar

All day digging the hole,
then later lowering your body, still
warm with sun and heart,
wanting to join you down
deep in the earth's brown pelt.
I dug you the most beautiful hole
filled with forsythia.
When grandpa's old wood shovel broke
I got down to scoop the field dirt,
rocks, tear out the roots
while you watched. You, the long
walk up the slate mountain,
the swim across the high March river.
We lived large, every day of sautéed
butter and salt. You ran away
so many times in your wildness.
Always I got you back. I swear
that was you I saw when I drove
back to the city, coyote shimmering
by the roadside staring straight at me.
It rained as I made a ring of stones
on top of your grave, and the wind
blew a hole right through me
in the shape of a dog running
on my first night without you.

Shoebox Diorama

Here is the elk-yard, tamped down,
frozen with tunnels like my own ice brain, white and secret.
I make a crown of sheds to wear the sky antlered.
In my kingdom barges no longer pull their dark payloads
downriver. Cities shrink and furl in the bonsai metropolis.
Forests spread their glamour of beasts.
Waters are clear and whale-full.
Dams break open. Extinct river dolphins return,
blind and lustrous under the curved light cast by minor planets.
I water the box every day—it is easy to care.

Intima

To make a home for each breath
we model a room of glass
walls veined from fall's red leaves.
A body turned inside out to house us.
Here we can think of the boats with eyes
slant at the prows to see the catch,
face storm, carry the travelers
to refuge, stare down the sea
when it comes to take back.
In this room things can happen.
Loss suspends its long rope
across disappointment to grace.
Your eyes our first night together.
Their gaze, the wet pearl
necklace rising above the sheets,
wearing us together.

Music for Surrender

High up, god in a tree looking owl small,
surveying the ribcage, the white fires of a brief life.
Tomorrow will be a decisive victory
for someone with form severe, form cold-blooded.
Where did the war go?
Asleep, gone to acres of lace.
Slowly and with care, I put my feet on
the ground, mud on my shoes.
There is not enough room in the world for the world.

Giant

I am going back to look at the body.
I forget how many it has killed
or if it had a wife, a child, a husband.
By now I have contained the enemy
so long I have become the enemy.
The best rampart is one of men.
I put on the steel helmet.
The gleam of my metal cooking pot
betrays me. My heirs will know me
by the content of my stomach.
Seeds will rise from the earth
as fields of ancient grain.
I have gathered all the light
of a lifetime so I can see in the dark.

Pavane

To tell the whole truth of the dream
of the sword, homemade and no need

of a shield, cut from cardboard and laid
across the spell of long hair. Help me, mother,

to defend what is me
carved in the sound of large birds dying.

We move slowly into the music, toes lifted
while the babble of the end flows beneath.

Now is the time for us to dip our tresses
in the sea and take away its oil.

Now to dance the dance of the real horse
and the fake horse, of the farmer

and the field, of the sticks and handkerchiefs,
of burying our general and marching

over his body, when all will be
as it was before human hands.

Notes

"The Lace Makers" is based on the letters between Albert Einstein and Max Born, and the writings of Hadewijch, the thirteenth-century mystic Beguine.

"Counterspell" takes inspiration from the sculpture of Diana Cherbuliez.

The title of "Abstraction Is Enchanted Ground and I Have Something Terrible to Paint Before Harvest Time" is based on a Vincent van Gogh letter to Émile Bernard in which he refers to abstraction as enchanted ground.

Sakuramochi is a Japanese confection made with sweetened pink rice, red bean paste and cherry leaf.

"Minotaur, Moving" refers to a Picasso painting called *Minotaur Moving His House*.

The title of "Piranesian Space" is inspired by Giovanni Battista Piranesi's series of etchings of imaginary prisons.

Kitsunetsuki is a Japanese word describing the state of being possessed by a fox. The poem is occasioned by the Yoshitoshi print of the Fox-Woman Kuzunoha.

"Christina's World" is named after the painting by Andrew Wyeth.

Acknowledgments

I want to thank Mekeel McBride for selecting this book for the May Sarton New Hampshire Poetry Prize. Deep gratitude to Lucie Brock-Broido. My warm thanks to Augusta Alvarez, Catherine Barnett, Claudia Burbank, Jenny Goodman, James Hallett, Carol Howell, Stephen Massimilla, Jaime Permuth, Julia Reidhead, Maddy Rosenberg, Helen Klein Ross, Jo Sarzotti, Gail Segal, Karen Steinmetz, Mac Wellman, and Catherine Woodard. Grateful acknowledgment to Bauhan Publishing for publishing my first book, and to Poets House and the Lower Manhattan Cultural Council Workspace Program for their support. I cherish and am graced by the many extraordinary personal friendships that have enriched my life and my writing. Michel Franck, thank you for your inspiration.

Thank you to the editors of the following journals in which these poems first appeared:

Best American Poetry blog: "Familiar"
Black Renaissance Noire: "Ingenue," "Ingenue 2," "Pilgrimage," "Restaging the Battle of the Little Bighorn," "Scrapyard," "Vagabonding"
Boston Review: "Grace"
Denver Quarterly: "Attributes of Speed," "The Inside of My Mouth"
Ellen Laforge Prize chapbook: "Aria," "Blood Mandala," "Minotaur, Moving "
The Iowa Review: "The Art of Bell Ringing," "Djinn," "Pavane"
Poetry: "The Order in Which Things Are Broken"
Poets House website: "Echolocation"
Prairie Schooner: "Abstraction Is Enchanted Ground and I Have Something Terrible to Paint Before Harvest Time," "Early Explorer's Journal"

The May Sarton New Hampshire Poetry Prize

The May Sarton New Hampshire Poetry Prize is named for May Sarton, the renowned novelist, memoirist, poet, and feminist (1912–1995) who lived for many years in Nelson, New Hampshire, not far from Peterborough, home of William L. Bauhan Publishing. In 1967, she approached Bauhan and asked him to publish her book of poetry, *As Does New Hampshire*. She wrote the collection to celebrate the bicentennial of Nelson, and dedicated it to the residents of the town.

May Sarton was a prolific writer of poetry, novels, and perhaps what she is best known for—nonfiction on growing older (*Recovering: A Journal, Journal of Solitude*, among others). She considered herself a poet first, though, and in honor of that and to celebrate the centenary of her birth in 2012, Sarah Bauhan, who inherited her father's small publishing company, launched the prize. (www.bauhanpublishing.com/may-sarton-prize)

PAST MAY SARTON WINNERS:

In *The Wreck of Birds*, the first winner of Bauhan Publishing's May Sarton New Hampshire Poetry Prize, Rebecca Givens Rolland embraces an assimilation of internal feeling and thought with circumstances of the natural world and the conflicts and triumphs of our human endeavors. Here, we discover a language that seeks to at once replicate and transcend experiences of loss and disaster, and together with the poet "we hope that such bold fates will not forget us." Even at the speaker's most vulnerable moments, when "Each word we'd spoken / scowls back, mirrored in barrels of wind" these personal poems insist on renewal. With daring honesty and formal skill, *The Wreck of Birds* achieves a revelatory otherness—what Keats called the "soul-making task" of poetry.

—Walter E. Butts, New Hampshire Poet Laureate (2009–2013), and author of *Cathedral of Nervous Horses: New and Selected Poems,* and *Sunday Evening at the Stardust Café*

Rebecca Givens Rolland is a speech-language pathologist and doctoral student at the Harvard Graduate School of Education. Her poetry has previously appeared in journals including *Colorado Review, American Letters & Commentary, Denver Quarterly, Witness, and the Cincinnati Review,* and she is the recipient of the Andrew W. Mellon Fellowship, the Clapp Fellowship from Yale University, an Academy of American Poets Prize, and the Dana Award.

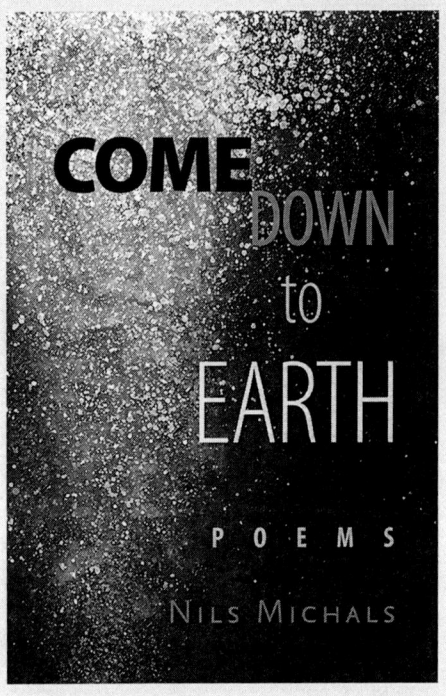

Nils Michals won the second May Sarton New Hampshire Poetry Prize in 2012, and has also written the book *Lure*, which won the Lena-Miles Wever Todd award in 2004. His poetry has been featured in *The Bacon Review*, *diode*, *White Whale Review*, *Bay Poetics*, *The Laurel Review* and *Sonora Review*. He lives in Santa Cruz, California and teaches at West Valley College.

Nils Michals is alternately healed and wounded by the tension between the timeless machinations of humankind and the modern machinery that lifts us beyond—and plunges us back to—our all-too-human, earthly selves. Supported by minimally narrative, page-oriented forms, his poems transcribe poetry's intangibles—love, loss, hope, a sense of the holy—in a language located somewhere between devotional and raw, but they mourn and celebrate as much of what is surreal in today's news as of what is familiar in the universal mysteries . . . *Come Down to Earth* is a 'long villa with every door thrown open' "

—Alice B. Fogel, New Hampshire Poet Laureate (2014-2019), and author of *Strange Terrain: A Poetry Handbook for The Reluctant Reader* and *Be That Empty*

David Koehn won the third May Sarton New Hampshire Poetry Prize in 2013. His poetry and translations were previously collected in two chapbooks, *Tunic*, (speCt! books 2013) a small collection of some of his translations of *Catullus*, and *Coil* (University of Alaska, 1998), winner of the Midnight Sun Chapbook Contest. He lives with his family in Pleasanton, California.

David Koehn's first book, *Twine*, never falters—one strong poem after another. This is the work of a mature poet. His use of detail is not only precise and evocative; it's transformative."
—JEFF FRIEDMAN,
2013 May Sarton New Hampshire Poetry Prize judge and author of *Pretenders*

David Koehn's imagination, rambunctious and abundant, keeps its footing: a sense of balance like his description of fishing: "Feeling the weight . . . of the measurement of air." That sense of weight and air, rhythm and fact, the ethereal and the brutal, animates images like boxers of the barefist era: "Hippo-bellied/And bitter, bulbous in their bestiary masks." An original and distinctively musical poet.

—ROBERT PINSKY,
United States Poet Laureate, 1997-2000
and author of *Selected Poems,* among numerous other collections

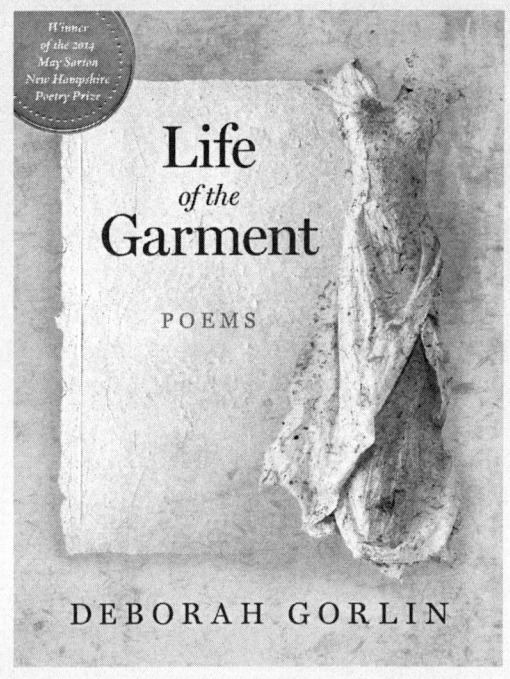

Deborah Gorlin won the 2014 May Sarton New Hampshire Poetry Prize. She has published in *Poetry, Antioch Review, American Poetry Review, Seneca Review, The Massachusetts Review, The Harvard Review, Green Mountains Review, Bomb, Connecticut Review, Women's Review of Books, New England Review,* and *Best Spiritual Writing 2000.* Gorlin also won the 1996 White Pine Poetry Press Prize for her first book of poems, *Bodily Course.* She holds an MFA from the University of California/Irvine. Since 1991, she has taught writing at Hampshire College, where she serves as co-director of the Writing Program. She is currently a poetry editor at *The Massachusetts Review.*

In poem after poem in *Life of the Garment,* Deborah Gorlin clothes us in her fabric of sung words, with characters unique and familiar, and facsimiles of love that open and close their eyes, comfort, and gaze upon us. Read this fine collection—you will see for yourself.

—Gary Margolis, 2014 May Sarton New Hampshire Poetry Prize judge and author of *Raking the Winter Leaves.*